MW01256618

To Mayo...,

Happy Birthday

all The

Best,

D told Puckler

2010

the Angina Dialogues

Poems by
Dr. Sidney Rosenblum, DC

Library of Congress Number: 2008923216

© 2008 Dr. Sidney Rosenblum. All rights reserved.

Cover and Interior design by Bobby Dawson

This book may not be reproduced in any form without express written permission.
Printed in the United States of America
ISBN 978-1-58385-236-1
ISBN 1-58385-236-0

Dedicated To Marcia Jean.

When I see my wife
She is as fresh as a
Kindergarten kid
Her voice as eager
As the beginning of day
Shadows pass through
Her heart
And leave as sunlight.

FOREWORD

This collection of poems by Sidney Rosenblum offers many delights to anyone interested in the struggle of the human mind to transcend pain and create beauty and art. There are occasional poems, epigrams, and many simple, brief poems that allow us to see ordinary events and circumstances in unanticipated ways. Throughout, we sense that we are exposed to a mind that strips away all artifice and pretense in pursuit of that which is authentic. A central concern is the ability to overcome anxiety in order to revel in the potential pleasures of life. We come to know that we are in a land dominated by courage and truthfulness.

If one believed in such a thing as "poetry therapy," this collection would provide an excellent example of the process. Many of the poems illustrate the neurotic process of symptom formation in reverse: an associative link of images travels from the symptom back to deeper layers of affect and memory. We can see this process illustrated poignantly in "The Doctor Visit" as the agoraphobic awareness of traveling to a doctor is peeled down to reveal more affect-laden fantasies. The poems travel from affect to memory and back.

The poems are richly evocative and piercingly honest. "Things When You Get Old" is wise and empathic in its earnest listing of subjective experiences: the allusions ring true. "Second Avenue Deli" demonstrates the depth of Rosenblum's connection both to his own subjective experiences and to elements in his environment. Poems like "To a Once Dear Friend" and "Tough" make us aware of the poet's vulnerability and continual struggle to achieve a livable inner peace. We get the sense that, if we stay around, we are near a source of wisdom and love.

David Lerner, MSW, Psychoanalyst
New York City

From The Desk Of

The Angina Dialogues represents a true insight into the heart and soul of a healer. This physician's feelings pour out onto the pages with emotion, intellect, and a deep understanding of the human psyche. It's as if the doctor's very existence is dependent upon writing down his thoughts. As Dr. Rosenblum himself says, "My poems write themselves."

Each poem brings one into the mind of this creative writer sensing his visual and visceral ability to hit straight at the heart of the matter.

My favorite poem is called "Sooner or Later." The doctor tells us that everyone we meet in life ends up in our dreams. After all, as Chuang Tzu once said, "Am I a man who dreamed I was a butterfly or a butterfly dreaming I am a man? Perhaps my whole life is but a moment in a butterfly's dream."

This spectacular set of poems is a must read for all physicians, dreamers, and true romantics.

Sincerely,
Louis V. Angioletti, MD, FACS

AUTHOR'S NOTE

The poems I write seem to find me. When I take the time to listen, they write themselves. They are written without time—energy without a clock. My poems are snapshots of my real self: the unguarded, feeling, and thinking part of me. They write themselves out of chaos and a desire for clarity. Reality is there, like a painting beneath a painting.

After writing a poem, it's as if I have awakened from a sleep, refreshed, renewed, and able to deal with the conflicts that catalyzed the writing.

For me, psychotherapy and writing are extensions of each other. The muse and the subconscious are married. Together, they encourage the abilities to listen to and let what is going on inside, emerge. A new child, a new universe may come into being.

I have been writing poems for fifty years. My poems have become like trusted friends, passports from alien landscapes to emotions that eluded awareness. They have carried me through adolescence, love, marriage, fatherhood, career, and aging.

My poems have served me well. I hope they will also serve you.

Sidney Rosenblum

CONTENTS

the Angina Dialogues

THE CHIROPRACTOR

My fingers become
My eyes
The spinal
Muscles reveal
Their stories
Grief and gravity
I scan the breathing
Instruct inhalation
Exhalation
The spirit
Trapped inside
These sinews
Memories
Embodied in posture
The adjustment
Finally
The release.

TEARS

Tears
Are really blood
Tears
Feed the soul
Opposite of anger
Have you cried today?
Not in anguish
But from joy
Our tears are memories
They carry our history
Reminding us of who we are.

TOUGH

I tried to be tough
My whole life
A bullet
I discovered I was a reed
In a wooden flute
I took in anger like a thirsty plant
Now I weep
Stronger than any bullet.

ANGER, RAGE, AND FEAR

Anger, rage, and fear are the costumes
We wear
Shame
Our undergarments.

SHAME

I believe
Certain acts of behavior
Are crimes
That go unrecorded
Like dancers on the dance floor
They bump into you
And leave their painful imprint
Certain acts of behavior
Have their logic
In the perpetrator's narcissism
They leave you with a feeling of shame.

FEAR

I have a fear
The jacket I ordered online won't fit
I ordered the wrong one
I have a fear that I will be repetitive
Won't remember
I have a fear that I will be crushed
by my own thoughts
I have a fear that I will choke
on words not spoken
I have a fear that fear will
be my only excitement
I have a fear that I will grow
to love my fear
Like a trusted friend.

ANXIETY

I get anxious
I curl up like a snake
My blood turns cold
I hide from the world
I get anxious
The past is calling
To let me know
Who it thinks I am
I don't like it
It's familiar
I feel happiness
When it passes.

IT

When I am in touch with
It
I am not so upset
Confused
Hurt or disappointed
My journey is to find myself
Sometimes in the rubble of a friend's words
I am always looking for it
So embedded yet so elusive
Like smoke and fog on a clear day
It
Often painful
But numbness
Is worse
How not to postpone reality
Please tell me.

ENLIGHTENMENT

I woke up
Put the various nuts
In small individual jars
The quiet of the night
Except for the air conditioner
Helped me think
I am a fool
I know that about myself
The things I need to know
Other people can teach me
Enlightenment never stops
Staying awake.

CHICKEN SOUP

Ummm
What are you eating?
Chicken soup
You made chicken soup this morning?
Yeah
While you were complaining
Worrying about the future
I was chopping and measuring
It turned out very good
I chop and measure in my own way
You chop and measure
The same story
I am surprised there is any
Meat on the bones
Chicken soup I know
The future's not so sure
I have learned
You have got to eat
Worrying is optional.

A COAT OF TEARS

Enough
I told her
After a while
All you're wearing is
A coat of tears
That's what people will do to you
They will fit you for a tragic costume
I wear a coat of smiles
It keeps me going.

REJECTION

I know a guy who is a catalyst
For rejection
He instigates his own
Inflicts verbal wounds
Asks to be taken out to lunch
Guys like that can kill
First you take them seriously
Slowly
Reality emerges
It's so quiet without these semantic
Vultures
And yet they have their charms
Like the moths
Who return to the light.

I KNOW PEOPLE

I know people
Who can turn assumptions
Into facts
Projections into realities
I know people who take their sport
In attacking vulnerability
They think peace is in war
I try not to be one of them.

TO A ONCE DEAR FRIEND

Although you are not so dear at the moment
I am not angry with you
I could not endure
The pigheaded judgments of your words
Like fists lashing out.

We Used to Be Such Good Friends

Was it something I said
Or was it something you said
Or did?
I can't remember
I do remember we had only warm air
Between us
No chill or harsh wind of hurt
I suppose it is natural selection
That has brought us to this stand
It doesn't seem like intelligent design.

ENDINGS

The end of friendships
Cut deep into the heart
Hurts perceived or real
What happened?

DEAD ENEMIES

If all my enemies
Were dead
Would I create
New ones?
I'm sure
I'd get around to it
After a while.

E-MAIL TO MY GUT

5:20 a.m.
I received a message
From my gut
It spoke clearly
I don't have to be angry
All debts have been
Settled and paid
Stop rehearsing
The old sorrows
There will be new
Challenges.

JEWISH SINS

Each year I get to rid myself of my sins
I don't eat for twenty-four hours
When the sun goes down
My account is zero sins
I immediately collect new ones
I sin against myself
With thoughts of being hurt
With minor grudges
Penance for not noticing the moon.

YIDDISHLAND

I am from Yiddishland
Grown in the soil of Post-World War II
Brooklyn
Born of bagel and matzo brie
Mobsters and Rabbi
From Russia and Poland
Came my ancestors
Lebisch and Morris and Dora and Sam
Driven here by the Cossack wind
Landing in the settlements
Of Black Williamsburg
Twenty years later owning
The neighborhood
Yiddishland
The voices I hear
When I close my eyes
These clowns and actors
Capitalists who danced the rumba
Laughing and smiling
To them Happiness was a religion.

SECOND AVENUE DELI

In the place where corned beef was king
Now stands a Chase Manhattan Bank
Where currency mingles with
Aromas of knishes and kielbasa
Matzo ball soup
Safety deposit boxes
Have no blintzes in them
The memories of the
Jewish palette
Speak in brisket and pastrami
The Jewish heart created the cuisine that would
Give it a heart attack
Death was almost worth the meal
The comfort of potato salad
A hot dog with coleslaw
Where?
Gone.

Fantasy Road Trip

If I were to travel cross country
I would be driving
In the front seat
Lenny Bruce
In the backseat
Freud
My fantasy buddies
I would feel secure
Knowing Lenny would scream the truth
Sigmund would know the truth
The drive would be serene
Walt Whitman could be invited.

IF YOU WANT TO KNOW WHO I AM

If you want to know who I am
Refer to my subconscious
Talk to my mother
Talk to my father
Talk to my first love
It is too much trouble
To squabble over trifles
Kindly ask my subconscious
What it is thinking and feeling
And we will get along just fine.

WHEN I WAS A CHILD

When I was a child
There was a hill
It was very steep
And difficult to climb
I saw other kids tackle it
I have thought about that hill
For many years
Now being much older
I went back to see that hill
And can't understand
What seemed so difficult.

I Was Raw at 17

I could have been pulverized into emotional
Dust
Like chalk on a school board
So much dust now
Fifty years later
A visit from the raw youth
Demanding a full reading
I have kept this chap at bay
For as long as I could
Now he takes me
By the hand
And shows me
What is behind the screen
I am thankful for the strength
Of this raw youth
He has pulled me through all my fires
Passionate but incapable
I will let this raw youth
Be my guide.

SELF-PURSUIT

I went looking for a pair of glasses
And found myself
I heard a voice
Worth listening to
And found it was mine
I saw a man in the street
Whose fist was clenched in anger
I walked up to him
And asked if I could help
Slowly I pried each finger open
And soothed his hand
It had turned blue like his heart
Painfully he smiled and thanked me
I woke up and saw my hand open.

GOOD NIGHT

When I fall asleep
I see myself
Not as a stranger
But someone
Worth knowing.

CRAZY PERSON

Ever see a crazy person
Walking down the street
Muttering
Flailing
Most of us
Act that way
Only in a more subdued
Fashion
We hide our scenarios of pain
Speaking in barely audible
Tones
Not to disturb
Or draw attention to
Our unresolved feelings
Finding a border at
The outer edges
What stops our madness?

AFTERNOON MAN

I saw a man this afternoon
Walking across the park
Dragging himself through space
Every step forward
An invisible grimace
I knew the man
He looked as if life was a war
I wanted to call out
I waited
He passed
And the moment
Passed with him.

Subway Dreams

My worst dreams
Take place in subway cars
Shoeless
Begging for direction
Looking for my station
Never arriving at my destination.

EVERYONE HAS A SADNESS

Everyone has a sadness
The thing that makes them grey
Washes out the color
Puts a crack in every voice
Everyone has the what to hide from
A truth behind the wall
Everyone has a sound too hard to make
A shadow they cannot break
Everyone has a person who has killed them
Without a death
Given them a morning without sun
A night without end
Everyone has the life they carry
That makes love difficult
Everyone.

SOONER OR LATER

Sooner or later
Everyone you have known
Ends up in your dreams
All our laughter and tears
Have come from someone
Who has spoken to you
They are all there
In your dreams
And you
In theirs
Waiting.

THE EMPTY CHILD

The empty child
A leaf
Torn from a branch.

MEN HAVE BROKEN HEARTS

If they stop to listen
The words of men would be
Gentle after they scream
The words in men's heads
Can be the cure.

THE OLD SORROWS

Unwelcome guests refuse to leave
And yet we serve them tea
As if they were our masters.

AMAZED

I am amazed
That some people
Know me better than
They know themselves.

DEPRESSION

Depression
The quiet scourge
Implosion
Of body mind
Internal traffic
Misdirected
Fury
Without sound
Here
Most of the time
Anger is needed
The quiet obsession.

MIND BODY SPLIT

An old canard
The mind tries to control
Its destiny
Listen
The body will tell the mind
Which direction to row.

THE HEART SHOULD WIN

The heart should win
In every conversation
In every battle with the brain.

MEMORY

Looking for a sign
From the past
I see forged documents
Frozen words
Broken promises.

I COULD HAVE USED YOUR HELP

I am here putting myself together
With glue
I don't think about you now
At least I don't think I do
I could have used your help

WOULD YOU TALK TO SOMEONE WHO DOESN'T LISTEN?

Would you talk to someone
Who doesn't listen?
How would it make you feel?
Why do we do this?
I think it is because they
Don't listen
We want to hear an echo
Of understanding in our hearts
I think often
The people we need
To hear us
Cannot listen to themselves
Why do I talk to people
Who don't listen?
Maybe
In the childish hope
That they will
Hear me.

SUDDENLY I REALIZED

Suddenly I realized
How to forgive
Able now
To protect myself
Life gives me a chance
To put myself
Back together
My heart deaf
For a long time
Now waits
Now listens.

THE DOCTOR VISIT

There is the traveling there
It is not that far
Maybe a half hour
But going there for information
That may change your life
Perhaps it is already changed
And you received no notification
On the way there
A telegram from the past
Announcing your anxiety
Life has always been
Managing anxiety
The tension of language and memory
But today I will relax
And let what is going to happen
Happen.
As if I could stop it.

Blood Work

Tap, tap, tap, the hand raps the arm
White steel goes into the blue road
It is a lonely experience
Having your blood taken
Drawing out the truth of who you are
All your secrets drawn from a red well
How curiously we cling to life and pleasure
Looking from this side of death
Hoping the numbers and odds will favor you
But will those numbers grant you
The wisdom you seek
The honor you deserve?
The white steel
Draws out the substance of our ancestors
Our transgressions
But will not tell us
The secret of who we are.

THIS IS JUST FOR ME

I can enjoy it
I feel safe in it
No need to armor
No thoughts or words desecrate
Or intrude upon this peace
No conditions arbitrated
A deep breath
A sigh
A moment that is truth itself
Without argument
My senses continually renewed
This is infinity and yet I know
It ends like a rainbow bending
Toward an invisible arc
Just for me
An opening without a landscape
The hardest thing I've ever done
I came to the place
Where there are no symbols
This is just for me
It is my love for you.

LAST NIGHT DID NOT FEEL LIKE SLEEP

Last night did not feel
Like sleep
I was dreaming
Upside down
Walking through
An invisible door
Seeing the sun for the first time
My mind
Clear
The view
Unobstructed
Because you are here.

How I Found Out That I Loved You

At first when you left
I felt a chill
While you were gone
I listened to your voice message
I heard myself in your words
An animal recognizing
The scent
When in love
People
Become each other
As they say
For better
Or worse.

MAN AND WOMAN

Don't get upset
It's just me.

WHEN I WAS YOUNG

When I was young
I never saw old people
What I mean is I didn't look
Until I was closer to being old
The old belong to another race of people
It takes as much wisdom and grace
To grow into old age as it does into adulthood
Now my eye trains
On the distant approaching person
Who hobbles and struggles against gravity
With too numerous pains
I pass the elderly as if in slow motion
A mixture of empathy and dread
I recognize life's fingerprint
In the halting staccato walk
The elderly need as much as bewildered children
On the first day of school
The bent head mirroring resignation
I read the map of the body like a navigator
The physical and the spiritual
Living at last in the same body
I observe the elderly like rare coins
Hoping to gain some strategy to that place
Where I am going.

THINGS WHEN YOU GET OLD

Soaking my feet
Measuring distances
Bending
Twisting
Anger management
Coughing
Somewhere love is in here
The bathtub
Porcelain
Hard surfaces
Bikes on sidewalks
Seeing what I refused to see
This is the beginning.

HOPE AND DESPAIR

Things wind down
They disappear
When you're young
It's about hope
Age can bring despair
Emotional pain
Turns physical
Someone you relied on is
Gone.

GETTING OLD

Sometimes turning over in bed
Is not such a good idea
So casual a move can cause pain
Standing up can be tricky
The brain has the idea
The feet not always willing
Balance and memory
A juggling act
Some fences left behind
Broken.

REVISION

I can't revise my life
Living is a play
The characters
Have delivered their lines
I look in the wings
And hope
There is more logic
In the final act.

NOW WITH AGE

Now with age
Beauty is the serene
Pleasure
Enjoyed without the
Hunt
Who was the prey?
Who was the conquered?
At every age
We are taught
To quarrel with our
Souls
A truce before death
Victory.

HEART LAND

for John Coppola, MD

My heart is a camera;
it takes pictures even when I sleep.
It records time.
It records panic and misery and pain and love.
It never lies to me and pounds like a racehorse
when I treat it like an orphan.

My heart loves me, even when I ignore it–
that is what it does.
It helps me caress others,
protects me from myself.
It carries sunlight and fireflies.
It dances with dragonflies.

Our hearts should speak to each other
like deaf people sign,
but how can we ask what we so often deny?

The brain is an assembly line, the heart a carousel.
Everyday I have lunch with my heart;
we feed each other the truth and laugh
at our illusions.
We pray together
so that we may not end our days apart.

"Heart Land" first published in JAMA, 2007, volume 298, page 380. Copyright © (2007), American Medical Association. All Rights reserved.

ACKNOWLEDGMENTS

A remark, a word of encouragement, even criticism; all contribute to the creative process.

Here are some of the people who have nurtured and provoked the writing of my poems. I would like to thank: Howard V. Sann, of Victory Ink, for true and tested friendship and expert editorial marksmanship; my wife, Marcia Jean Kurtz, who made the journey possible with her red pencil, sharp eye, and loving heart. David Lerner, MSW, for assuring the safe passage of my unconscious; Gaby de Gail, my French connection, whose exquisite sensibility helped me believe in my words; the late writer Kay Boyle, who believed in my writing in the 1960s; Dr. John Coppola, cardiologist, who read my poem "Heart Land" and urged me to publish it; Charlene Breedlove, editor of the Journal of the American Medical Association (JAMA), who agreed to publish it and taught me to revise; Judy, Aaron, and Elena Banfield, my uniquely talented and creative Canadian family; Irving and Dora Kurtz for lasting memories of unconditional love; Linda Appleman Shapiro for her emotional strength and wit, and her husband, George Guidall, my contrarian muse who deconstructs

my poems into alternate universes; Robert Lapides for astute poetic direction; Miriam Chaikin for poetic guidance; Nancy and Ken Grimes for sensitive critiques; Goldie Kahn, lover and keeper of the Yiddish language; Barbara Hamilton, of spirit, heart, and mind; Iris Litt and Jerry Solk for poetic inspiration; Edward Field, the poet who became my patient; Barbara Wolver for seeing the merit in my work; Rachel Rippy, a positive voice; and Rachel Fichter of Cold Tree Press for creating the order of the poems to show the journey taken.

There are those who are there when you need them, who catch you when you fall, and listen when you laugh and cry. They include my loving sister, Gerry, and my brother, Artie, and my cousins Dahlia and Al Gutenberg, Suzie and Al Glick, Del and Ben Turgelsky; Francine, Bernie and Linda Rosenstein; Nira Levine of the Northwest, Ted and Roberta Plafker, our China connection; and Marjorie and Alice Kurtz and family.

Mark Segall for always being there; Gail Sicilia and Stanley Solson, great dinner conversationalists; Anita Picker, the apple of my eye; David and Cyrelle Soffer of Jerusalem and their magical, Middle Eastern daughters, Dina and Ruti; Janaan Simon; Debbie and Al Greco; Edna Cohen and family for warmth and friendship; Gil Raiford and family for staying in touch with this raw youth; Deborah Donnelly, always a positive force; John, Maria, and Grant Boller, good friends; Suzanne Skloot for support and friendship; Miriam and Richard Meisler

for endless friendship; Bruce R. Jaffe, friend and computer lifeguard; Harry, Clarissa, Hugo, and Gabriel Uvegi, quartet of beauty; Ronni Kolotkin and her "offspring," Diego and Frankie Avalon; John Mace and Richard Dorr of the vocal arts; Michael Tucker and Jill Eikenberry; Tovuh Feldshuh for being a special force of acknowledgment; Atticus, my little angelic friend; David Krouse, a true friend from California whom I will never forget for showing up at my wedding unannounced; Charlie Gilbert, teacher and standup comic (I'll always be your best man); Byron Tucker for karmic and economic expertise; Stewie Gubenko, CPA extraordinaire, who never taxed my friendship; and Rebecca Levine for human and legal wisdom; Mickey and Joan Rahav and family, for creating an oasis at Chelsmore, and Kumar, who keeps it going and The Kessler family, Lyle, Margaret, Michael and Katherine.

My amazing and caring doctors: Louis Angioletti, Bill Cook, John F. Romano, Joseph Sachs, and Jeffrey Wolfson; Robert Bard, a medical pioneer; James Robilotti for his great humor and diagnostic acumen; my friends and chiropractors, Mark Vincent and Larry August; Mark Bystock, acupuncturist; and my medical guru Robert M. Scholder.

Special thanks to Kaplan House of the Jewish Board of Guardians, in New York City, for adolescent restoration, and to Kaplan House Director Neil Freedman. May the Kaplan House residents and staff always see the horizon, because it is there.

To my mother, Fay, who has the biggest heart of all, and to the thousands of patients I have treated as a New York City chiropractor for the past thirty-five years—you have challenged my limits and expanded my horizons.

To the Chiropractic profession for what it has done to help me and for its gift to humanity.

Lastly–

To those who have gone, I send my love.

To those who remain, these poems are for you.

Sid Rosenblum, DC